# 50 Hymn Tunes
# Without Words For
# Sightreading

## With 20 Supplementary
## Bach Chorales

### Compiled by
# Donald L. Patterson, DMA

ISBN 1-58874-591-0

Published by

STIPES PUBLISHING L.L.C.
204 W. University Avenue
Champaign, Illinois  61820

# Introduction

Each of the hymn tunes is presented in two versions. First, only the soprano and bass lines are given. This provides a skeletal outline of the hymn and helps the student learn to read two parts fluently at the same time. Immediately following the 2-part version is the entire hymn presented with all four voices.

These hymns are arranged in order of difficulty. Those at the beginning of the book are easier than those at the end and the supplementary Bach Chorales are the most complicated of all. As the hymns progress, more accidentals, larger intervals, more frequent harmonic changes, and more crossing of voices are encountered. I placed only one hymn or chorale on each page to allow a font size that is easily readable and to help the learner focus.

In general hymn tunes are printed in keys that use no more than 4 flats or 4 sharps in the key signature. I have tried to provide as many different keys as seemed useful and have included hymns written in both major and minor keys.

The use of the pedal and the speed at which the hymns are read will depend on the skill level of the student and the directions provided by the teacher.

The words have been omitted from the hymns to allow the reader to concentrate on the purely pianistic problems of sightreading and manipulating the fingers. All of the hymns and chorales included in this volume were taken from the public domain.

An alphabetical list of hymn tunes names and sources is given at the end.

Good luck.

# Table of 50 Hymn Tunes for Sightreading

# 20 SUPPLEMENTARY BACH CHORALES

# Lubeck

Freylinghausen's "Gesangbuch"

## No. 1

# Lubeck 2

Freylinghausen's "Gesangbuch"

## No. 2

# Greenwell

William Kirkpatrick

## No. 3

# Greenwell 2

William Kirkpatrick

## No. 4

# Man of Sorrows

Philip Bliss

## No. 5

# Man of Sorrows 2

Philip Bliss

## No. 6

# St. Anne

Croft

## No. 7

# St. Anne 2

Croft

**No. 8**

# Winchester Old

Este

## No. 9

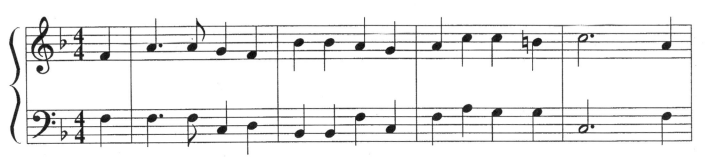

**5**

# Winchester Old 2

Este

## No. 10

# St. Michael

Genevan Psalter

## No. 11

# St. Michael 2

Genevan Psalter

## No. 12

# Sawley

James Walch

## No. 13

# Sawley 2

James Walch

## No. 14

# St. Agnes

John B. Dykes

## No. 15

# St. Agnes 2

John B. Dykes

## No. 16

# Italian Hymn

Giardini

## No. 17

# Italian Hymn 2

Giardini

## No. 18

# Unser Herrscher

Neander

## No. 19

# Unser Herrscher 2

Neandedr

## No. 20

# Truro

Psalmodia Evangelica

## No. 21

# Truro 2

Psalmodia Evangelica

# All Saints

Henry s. Cutler

## No. 23

# All Saints 2

Henry S. Cutler

## No. 24

# Lloyd

Cuthbert Howard

## No. 25

# Lloyd 2

Cuthbert Howard

## No. 26

# Manoah

Henry Greatorex Collection

**No. 27**

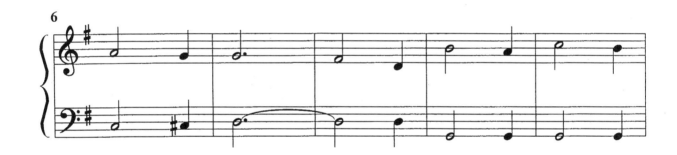

# Manoah 2

Henry Greatorex Collection

# St. Cuthbert

Johm B. Dykes

**No. 29**

# St. Cuthbert 2

John B. Dykes

## No. 30

# Virginia Harmony

Traditional American Melody

## No. 31

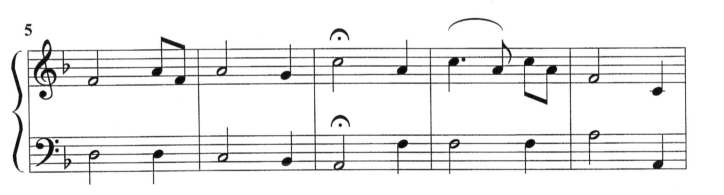

# Virginia Harmony 2

Traditional American Melody

## No. 32

# Quebec

Henry Baker

## No. 33

# Quebec 2

Henry Baker

## No. 34

# Sunset

George C. Stebbins

**No. 35**

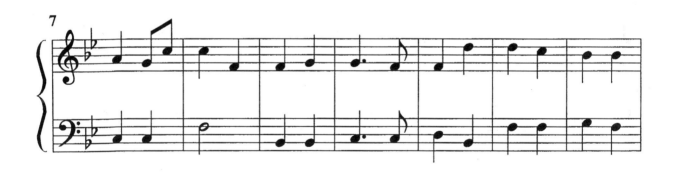

# Sunset 2

George C. Stebbins

## No. 36

# Schumann

Mason and Webb

### No. 37

# Schumann 2

Mason and Webb

## No. 38

# Dundee

Scottish Psalter

## No. 39

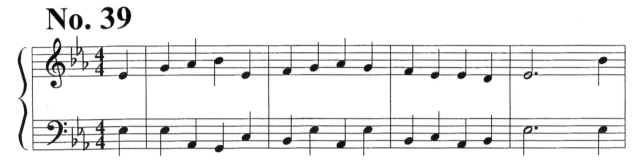

# Dundee

Scottish Psalter

## No. 40

# Mein Leben

Vulpius

## No. 41

# Mein Leben

Vulpius

## No. 42

# Spanish Chant

Anon

**No. 43**

# Spanish Chant 2

Anon

## No. 44

# Abridge

Isaac Smith

## No. 45

# Abridge 2

Isaac Smith

## No. 46

# Morecambe

Atkinson

## No. 47

# Morecambe 2

Frederick C. Atkinson 1870

## No. 48

# O Quanta Qualia

La Fellee

## No. 49

# O Quanta Qualia 2

La Fellee

**No. 50**

# Es ist ein Born

C. E. Miller

## No. 51

# Es ist ein Born 2

C. E. Miller

## No. 52

# Rockingham

Edward Miller

## No. 53

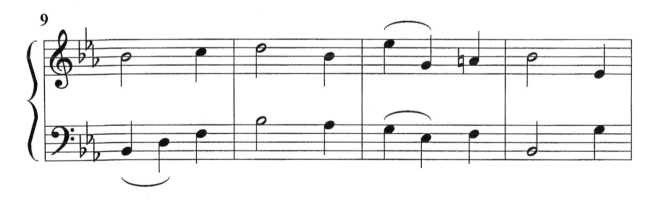

# Rockingahm 2

Edward Miller

# Lauda Anima

John Goss

**No. 55**

# Lauda Anima 2

John Goss

## No. 56

# Wer Nur den Lieben Gott

Neumark

## No. 57

# Wer nur den Lieben Gott 2

Neumark

## No. 58

# Seymour

von Weber

## No. 59

# Seymour

Weber/Wesley

## No. 60

# Nachtigall

Anthony Hedges

## No. 61

# Nachtigall 2

Anthony Hedges

## No. 62

# Bryn Calfaria

William Owen

## No. 63

# Bryn Calfaria 2

William Owen

# Mendebras

Old German Melody

## No. 65

# Mendebras 2

Old German Melody

## No. 66

# Russian Hymn

Alexis F. Lvov

## No. 67

# Russian Hymn 2

Alexis F. Lvov

## No. 68

# Slane

Irish Melody

## No. 69

# Slane 2

Irish Melody

**No. 70**

# Maccabaeus

George F. Handel

# Maccabaeus 2

George F. Handel

# Passion Chorale

Hassler

## No. 73

# Passion Chorale 2

Hassler

# Ein Feste Burg

Luther

## No. 75

# Ein Feste Burg 2

Luther

## No. 76

# Yigdal

Hebrew

## No. 77

# Yigdal 2

Hebrew

## No. 78

# Built on the Rock

Ludwig M. Lindman

# Built on the Rock 2

Ludvig M. Lindeman

**No. 80**

# Moville

Traditional Irish Melody

## No. 81

# Moville 2

Traditional Irish Melody

## No. 82

# Kingsfold

Traditional English Melody

## No. 83

# Kingsfold 2

Traditional English Melody

# O Filli et Fillae

15th Century French

# O Filli et Fillae 2

15th Century French

## No. 86

# St. Vincent

Sigismund Newkomm

**No. 87**

# St. Vincent 2

sigismund Newkomm

## No. 88

# Jesu, Meine Freude

Cruger

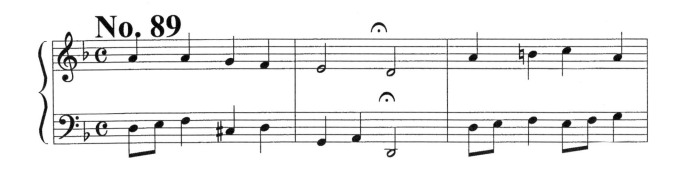

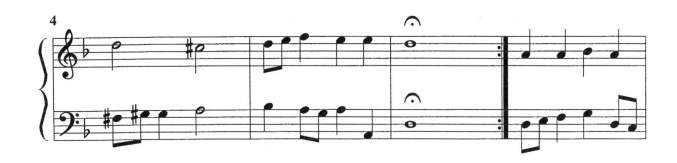

# Jesu, meine Freude 2

Cruger

# Abbyswyth

Joseph Parry 1879

**No. 91**

# Abbyswyth 2

Joseph Parry, 1879

# Mit Freuden Zart

Bohemian

**No. 93**

# Mit Freuden Zart 2

Bohemian

# Lux Benigna

John B. Dykes

**No. 95**

# Lux Benigna 2

John B. Dykes

# Lasst uns erfreuen

Gestliche Kirchengesang

**No. 97**

# Lasst uns Erfreuen 2

Geistliche Kirchegesang

No. 98

98

# Ebenezer

Thomas John Williams

# Ebenezer 2

Thomas John Williams

## No. 100

# 20 Supplementary Bach Chorales

# O du Liebe meiner Liebe

J. S. Bach

## No. 101

# Der Lieben Sonnen Licht und Pracht

J. S. Bach

## No. 102

# Lasset uns mit Jesu zichen

J. S. Bach

## No. 103

# Steh ich bei meinem Gott

J. S. Bach

## No. 104

# Die goldne Sonne, voll Freud' und Wonne

J. S. Bach

## No. 105

# Salzburg

J. S. Bach

## No. 106

# O Ewigkeit, du Donnerwort

Bach

# Pensum Sacrum

J. S. Bach

## No. 108

# O Haupt voll Blut und Wunden

J. S. Bach

No. 109

# Valet will ich dir geben

J. S. Bach

## No. 110

# Hast du denn, Jesu, dein Angesicht

J. S. Bach

**No. 111**

# Von Himmel Hoch

J. S. Bach

# Liebster Immanuel

J. S. Bach

## No. 113

# Aus Tiefer Not

J. S. Bach

# Frankfort

J. S. Bach

## No. 115

# Schop

J. S. Bach

## No. 116

# Ach Gott und Herr

J. S. Bach

No. 117

# Herr Gott, dich loben alle wir

J. S. Bach

# Jesu, Joy of Man's Desiring

J. S. Bach

## No. 119

# Wachet Auf

J. S. Bach

## No. 120

# Alphabetical List of Hymn Tunes and Chorale Titles

| TITLE | COMPOSER |
|---|---|
| Abbyswyth | Joseph Parry, 1879 |
| Abridge | Isaac Smith (1735-1800) |
| Ach Gott und Herr | J. S. Bach Cantata #48 |
| All Saints | Henry S. Cutler, 1872 |
| Aus Tiefer Not | J. S. Bach Cantata #38 |
| Built on the Rock | L. M. Lindeman(1812-1857) |
| Bryn Calfaria | William Owen (1814-1893) |
| Der lieben Sonnen Licht und Pracht | J. S. Bach *Zwansig Geistliche Lieder* |
| Die goldne Sonne, voll Freud' une Wonne | J. S. Bach *Zwansig Geistliche Lieder* |
| Dundee | Scottish Psalter, 1615 |
| Ebenezer | Thomas J. Williams, 1890 |
| Ein' Feste Burg | Martin Luther, 1529 |
| Es ist ein Born | C. E. Miller (1856-?) |
| Frankfort | J. S. Bach |
| Greenwell | W.Kirkpatrick (1838-1921) |
| Hast du denn, Jesu, dein Angesicht | J. S. Bach Cantata #57 |
| Herr Gott, dich loben alle wir | J. S. Bach |
| Liebster Immanuel | Himmels-Lust, 1675 |
| In Dulci jubilo | German Melody, 14th cent. |
| Italian Hymn | Felice de Giardini, 1769 |
| Jesu, Joy of Man's Desiring | Schop. Harm J. S. Bach |
| Jesu, Meine Freude | Johann Cruger, 1653 |
| Kingsfold | Trad. English Melody |
| Lasset uns mit Jesu zichen | J. S. Bach |
| Lasst uns Erfreuen | *Geistliche Kirchensgesäng* |
| Lauda Anima | John Goss, 1869 |
| Liebster Immanuel | Himmels-Lust, 1675 |
| Lloyd | C. Howard (1856-1927) |
| Lubeck | Freylinghausen, 1704 |
| Lux benigna | John B. Dykes, 1865 |
| Maccabaeus | G. F. Handel (1685-1759) |
| Man of Sorrows | Phillip Bliss (1838-1876) |
| Manoah | Henry W. Greatorez, 1851 |
| Mein Leben | Melchior Vulpius,1609 |
| Mendebras | Old German Melody, 1839 |

| | |
|---|---|
| Mit Freuden Zart | Bohemian Brethren's *Gesangbuch* |
| Morecambe | Frederick Atkinson, 1870 |
| Moville | Traditional Irish Melody |
| Nachtigall | von Spee, 1649 |
| O du Liebe meiner Liebe | J. S. Bach |
| O Ewigkeit, du Donnerwort | J. S. Bach Cantata #20 |
| O Filii et Filiae | French Melody 15th Cent. |
| O Haupt voll Blut und Wunden | J. S. Bach St. Matthew |
| O Quanta Qualia | La Feillée, 1808 |
| Passion Chorale | Hans Leo Hassler, 1601 |
| Pensum Sacrum | Görlitz, 1648 |
| Quebec | Henry Baker, 1854 |
| Rockingham | Edward Miller (1731-1807) |
| Russian Hymn | Alexis Lwoff, 1833 |
| St. Agnes | John B. Dykes, 1866 |
| St. Anne | William Croft, 1708 |
| St. Cuthbert | John B. Dykes (1823-1876) |
| St. Michael | Genevan Psalter, 1551 |
| St. Vincent | S. Newkomm (1779-1858) |
| Salzburg | Jakob Hintze (1622-1702) |
| Sawley | James Walch (1837-1901) |
| Schop | Johann Schop (1600-1665) |
| Schumann | Mason and Webb, 1850 |
| Seymour | Carl M. von Weber, 1826 |
| Slane | Traditional Irish, 1927 |
| Spanish Chant | Anon |
| Steh ich bei meinem Gott | J. S. Bach |
| Sunset | G. C. Stebbins (1846-1945) |
| Truro | T. Williams, 1789 |
| Unser Herrscher | J. Neander (1650-1680) |
| Valet will ich dir geben | J. S. Bach |
| Virginia Harmony | Traditional American |
| Von Himmel Hoch | Geistliche Lieder, 1539 |
| Wachet Auf | J. S. Bach Cantata #140 |
| Wer Nur den Lieben Gott | J. S. Bach Wedding Cant. |
| Winchester Old | Christopher Tye, 1553 |
| Yigdal | Hebrew Melody, 14th cent. |